This
*My First Communion Journal
In Imitation of St. Paul:
Putting on the Armor of God*
belongs to:

_____

Date of First Holy Communion:

_____

Place of First Holy Communion:

_____

_____

© 2011 by Janet P. McKenzie

ISBN 978-1-934185-43-8

Published by
Biblio Resource Publications, Inc.
108½ South Moore Street
Bessemer, MI 49911
www.BiblioResource.com
info@BiblioResource.com

All right reserved. With the exception of short excerpts for critical reviews, no part of this work may be reproduced or transmitted in any form or by any means whatsoever without the written permission of the publisher.

Cover photo © Joonarkan - Fotolia.com

Scripture texts in this work are taken from the *New American Bible with Revised New Testament* © 1986, 1970 Confraternity of Christian Doctrine, Washington, D.C. and are used by permission of the copyright owner. All Rights Reserved. No part of the *New American Bible* may be reproduced in any form without permission in writing from the copyright owner.

A **R**ead **A**loud **C**urriculum **E**nrichment Product
www.RACEforHeaven.com

Printed in the United States of America

General Instructions

(Note: If this journal is being used in conjunction with *Communion with the Saints, A Family Preparation Program for First Communion and Beyond in the Spirit of St. Therese,* be sure to read pages vi through viii in the "General Instructions" of that resource.)

This journal has been constructed in imitation of the "copybooks" used by Celine and Therese Martin as they prepared for their First Holy Communion in 1880 and 1884. These journals were lovingly made by Sr. Agnes of Jesus, the older sister of Celine and Therese Martin, who was at the time a Carmelite nun in the monastery at Lisieux, France. The homemade journals were described in a letter from Sr. Agnes to Therese as copybooks or "little books of preparation" where, under the symbols of flowers, the girls could record their sacrifices and pious thoughts. St. Therese's journal had a cover of blue velvet with her initials embroidered in large white letters. Inside was ". . . one page for each day. Each page was decorated with a border, rays in each of the corners, the date in Gothic illumination, the name of a flower and a short aspiration which the scent of the flower symbolized; it was all done in black and red ink. . . . Prayers to the Child Jesus, the Blessed Virgin, St. Joseph, and the guardian angel preface each of the. . . months."

During her preparation period, Therese was encouraged to turn her heart often to Jesus by reciting the prayers and aspirations in the copybook and to take every opportunity to humble her pride and make sacrifices for the good Jesus. Throughout her sixty-nine day preparation period, she recorded each day the number of times she recited the prayers and, by use of her "sacrifice beads" (a small chaplet of moveable beads—

for which directions are provided at the end of this book), she counted each time she overcame her own desires in order to please Jesus.

Therese herself, in her letter to Sr. Agnes thanking her for the copybook, tells us the importance she placed in this preparation for Holy Communion: "Every day, I try to perform as many practices as I can, and I do all in my power not to let a single occasion pass by. I am saying at the bottom of my heart the little prayers as often as I can."

At the end of her preparation period, Therese recorded that she had recited the aspirations a total of 2,773 times (an average of about 40 each day) and had performed 1,949 "practices" or little acts of mortification and sacrifice, for an average of 28 each day.

This journal contains the same method of encouraging continual daily prayer and sacrifice—and recording their numbers—as the copybook St. Therese used. However, instead of using flowers to illustrate virtues, this journal uses the battle model described by St. Paul in Ephesians 6:10-17. First communicants are encouraged to arm themselves with virtues as symbolized by spiritual and physical weapons in order to fight as soldiers of Christ.

I pray that this modern-day "copybook" will bring about the same results that the "little book of preparation" produced in the soul of little Therese so many years ago: the desire to please Jesus in every thought, word, and deed, thereby joining St. Paul's "holy ones" (Ephesians 6:18) in heaven.

Janet P. McKenzie, OCDS
November 18, 2011
Feast of the Dedication of the Churches of
Sts. Peter and Paul

Prayers and Aspirations

("For me, *prayer* is an aspiration of the heart, it is a simple glance directed to heaven." – St. Therese)

TO THE CHILD JESUS: (from the copybook of St. Therese)
- ✝ "Little Jesus, I love You,"
- ✝ "Little Jesus, don't let me be proud anymore."
- ✝ "Little Jesus, may I always be simple and docile."
- ✝ "My whole heart is Yours, Jesus."

TO THE BLESSED VIRGIN:
- ✝ "Holy Mary, help me, like you, to hold Jesus close to my heart."
- ✝ Remember, O most gracious Virgin Mary, that never was it known that anyone who fled to thy protection, implored thy help, or sought thy intercession was left unaided. Inspired by this confidence, I fly unto thee, O Virgin of virgins, my mother; to thee do I come, before thee I stand, sinful and sorrowful. O Mother of the Word Incarnate, despise not my petitions, but in thy mercy hear and answer me. Amen.
- ✝ "O Mary, conceived without sin, pray for us!"

TO ST. JOSEPH:
- ✝ "Dear St. Joseph, teach me to love Jesus as you did."
- ✝ "St. Joseph, foster-father of Jesus, pray for us."

TO MY GUARDIAN ANGEL:
- ✝ "Angel dear, guard and guide me."

(Note: Within the daily meditations are numerous other aspirations that can be prayed.)

My First Communion Journal

St. Paul: Putting on the Armor of God

"Put on the armor of God so that you may be able to stand firm against the tactics of the devil. For our struggle is not with flesh and blood but with the principalities, with the powers, with the world rulers of the present darkness, with the evil spirits in the heavens. Therefore, put on the armor of God, that you may be able to resist on the evil day and, having done everything, to hold your ground. So stand fast with your loins girded in truth, clothed with righteousness as a breastplate, and your feet shod in readiness for the gospel of peace. In all circumstances, hold faith as a shield, to quench all [the] flaming arrows of the evil one. And take the helmet of salvation and the sword of the Spirit, which is the word of God."

Ephesians 6: 10-17

Read-Aloud Story

The following story is Chapter 8, "The King's Armory," from *The King of the Golden City Study Edition,* a reprint of a book by Mother Mary Loyola originally published in 1921. Here, the little girl Dilecta is taken before the King so He can prepare her for battle against the world, her Self, and the devil (Malignus). Note the various weapons she is given on her Confirmation and their recommended uses.

You may be surprised that the youngsters had to fight so soon. But trying out their strength is a thing children take to very readily, and the worse the war is, the younger are the soldiers who are called out to fight. The war between the King of the Golden City and Malignus, the traitor, was the deadliest you can imagine, because if a soldier did not come out victorious in the end, there was no trying again for him. So the children, girls as well as boys, had to be taught well, and taught young. It was wonderful how grandly some of them fought, how soon they got promoted, and how afraid of them their cunning old enemy came to be.

One day Dilecta was summoned to the King's Presence. She was so accustomed to go to him without ceremony that she was rather frightened when the Prince Guardian told her she must kneel before him and listen very attentively to what he was going to say. Not without trembling, she knelt down—the Prince standing reverently at her right hand.

"My child," said the King, "you are now old enough to be enrolled in my Army. Malignus is getting fiercer and more cunning, and what he cannot do by himself, he is going to employ others to do for him. You are beginning to listen to people who are not on my side, who are not afraid of breaking my laws, and who laugh at my servants who try to keep these laws. Besides these enemies without, you have Self always with you. She is growing fast and getting stronger and bolder. You must grow stronger, too, so that you may be able to stand your ground and fight more bravely than you have done yet. I never send anyone to fight without providing a proper outfit. The Prince Guardian will take you to the Armory and get the equipment you need."

She was delighted and went off, asking questions all the way.

The Armory was a wonderful place. There you could see the weapons of many a brave soldier who had laid aside his arms only when the fight was fought and won, and the palm of victory had been placed in his hand instead. The Prince Guardian took her in and out among the war trophies, and explained to her why they were treasured there. Here was the sword of St. Ignatius of Loyola, which he himself hung up in the house of God to show he was going to be, from now on, a solider of the King of kings alone. Over against it was the shield of St. Joan of Arc, the brave maid who fought for God and for her country.

Dilecta was immensely interested in all she saw—swords and shields, helmets and breastplates, and—shoes! She managed to make out the inscriptions:

On the sword—"Faith." On the shield—"Trust in God." On the helmet—"Prayer." On the breastplate—"Mistrust of Self." On the shoes—"Patience and Perseverance."

"I think, Prince," she observed, "the shield and the breastplate are much the same."

"At least, they must always go together, Dilecta. 'Mistrust of Self' without 'Confidence in God' means discouragement—the beginning of all harm as you have discovered."

"What a lot of helmets there are, more than I could count."

"Yes, for every victory is won by 'Prayer.' Never suppose you can fight all by yourself. Ask for help quickly, the moment you see your enemy."

Read-Aloud Story

"Look at all the shoes! Soldiers don't fight with them; what are they there for?"

"To show that 'Patience and Perseverance,' in plodding on day after day, are necessary for every warrior. Opportunities of bringing the enemy down by a well-directed shot do not come every day, nor does the need of meeting him with sword and shield in open fight. But every day there is the toilsome march, the same dull round of duty, the hardships inseparable from life at the front. It is the constant trudging of weary feet that, more than anything else, brings a man to victory and reward."

So Dilecta was measured for her equipment, and it was made to fit her exactly. And when all was ready, her Prince Guardian led her before the King and his Court. And she knelt down before them all and placed her little joined hands within the hands of the King, and promised to be a good soldier and faithful to him. Then she was solemnly enrolled in the regular Army and given a mark by which everyone would know that she was now a soldier. That mark would be a disgrace should she turn out a traitor to the King, but a sign of distinction and glory if she remained faithful to him and fought his battles bravely.

Sword and shield and helmet and breastplate and shoes—he gave them all to her. Moreover, he promised that whatever help she wanted, she should have the minute it was needed, if only she asked for it. At the end of the ceremony, he gave her a little stroke on the cheek, not to hurt, but just to remind her that she must expect to suffer in his cause. Her three enemies would now be more than ever on the lookout for her, and as a soldier commanded to stand at "attention," she must be always on the alert.

Two of these enemies, Malignus and Self, you know. They were like hand and glove and generally worked together. The King was speaking of the third enemy when he said Malignus had accomplices, or helpers, who did for him what he could not do by himself. They were men, women, and even children, who could not wait for the good things of the Golden City. They said they wanted their good things now. "The time of our life," they said, "is short and tedious like the passing of a shadow. Come, therefore, and let us enjoy the good things that are present. Let us crown ourselves with roses before they are withered. Let us eat and drink, for tomorrow we die."

These people hated hard work and made trouble of every sort. All they cared about was eating and drinking, dress and amusement, pleasure of every kind. They wanted to be as comfortable as money could make them —to be admired, praised, and honored. They called themselves the "Jolly Ones," but their real name was "The Triflers."

"How will I know them?" said Dilecta to her Prince Guardian. "I know Malignus and I know Self by what they say and do, but how will I know the Triflers?"

"In the same way—by what they say, and what they do, and what they care about. All their talk is about the good things of the Land of Exile, and all they care about is to please and amuse themselves. They do nothing to deserve the rewards of the King of the Golden City and have no fear of displeasing him. So far from trying to serve him, they do all they can to turn others from his service and to make them forsake the narrow, uphill way, which is the King's highway. They try to draw his servants into the broad way that belongs to Malignus and leads to his place. Beware of them. They are doing the work of their master, and if you go with them, you will grow like them, and will share their fate."

MY FIRST COMMUNION JOURNAL IN IMITATION OF ST. PAUL: PUTTING ON THE ARMOR OF GOD

Daily Journal Entries

Week 1

> "In two and a half months, Jesus will come down into your heart for the first time! What a lot of work there is to do . . . and how little time there is to do it in!"
>
> Sr. Agnes (Pauline) to her sister Therese upon delivery of her "copybook"

I Pray Today: #_____

Day 1

My Battles Today:

_____
_____
_____
_____
_____
_____
_____

My Sacrifices Today: #_____

_____
_____
_____
_____
_____
_____

Week 1

> As a Christian, you live in a hostile world, a world full of dangerous and mighty enemies of your soul. As you go forth to battle this world, you must use the tools of armor that God and our Church provide you. As a soldier of Christ, you will encounter many enemies of your soul. Therefore, *". . . Let us then throw off the works of darkness [and] put on the armor of light"* (Romans 13:12).

I Pray Today: #_____

_____
_____
_____
_____
_____

Day 2

My Battles Today:
_____
_____
_____
_____
_____
_____

My Sacrifices Today: #_____
_____
_____
_____
_____
_____
_____

Week 1

> *"Put on the armor of God so that you may be able to stand firm against the tactics of the devil."*
> (Ephesians 6:11)

I Pray Today: #_____

_____
_____
_____
_____
_____

Day 3

My Battles Today:

My Sacrifices Today: #_____

Week 1

> You must stand firm, armed with the *"weapons of righteousness"* (2 Corinthians 6:7), *"For our struggle is not with flesh and blood but with the principalities, with the powers, with the world rulers of this present darkness, with the evil spirits in the heavens."* (Ephesians 6:12)

I Pray Today: #_____

Day 4

My Battles Today:

My Sacrifices Today: #_____

Week 1

> Soldiers of Christ, arise
> And gird your armor on;
> Eternal life the prize
> To be by victors won.
> The Cross shall give you might
> To scare the hellish foe;
> Equipped thus for the fight
> In God's name forward go.

I Pray Today: #_____

_____
_____
_____
_____
_____

Day 5

My Battles Today:
_____
_____
_____
_____
_____
_____

My Sacrifices Today: #_____
_____
_____
_____
_____
_____
_____

Week 1

> The first and most powerful weapon in Christ's armor of light is the SHIELD of **FAITH** with which you may extinguish all the fiery darts of the devil. Faith is an impenetrable shield against the temptations and snares of the devil. *"In all circumstance, hold faith as a shield, to quench all [the] flaming arrows of the evil one."* (Ephesians 6:16)

I Pray Today: #_____

_____
_____
_____
_____
_____
_____

Day 6

My Battles Today:

My Sacrifices Today: #_____

Week 1

> The pearl of great price (Matthew 13:45-46) is the true **FAITH** and the state of grace. Guard this treasure carefully. Sacrifice everything to preserve your faith. *"... Amen, I say to you, if you have faith the size of a mustard seed, you will say to this mountain, 'Move from here to there,' and it will move. Nothing will be impossible for you.'"* (Matthew 17:20)

I Pray Today: #____

_____

_____

_____

_____

_____

Day 7

My Battles Today:

My Sacrifices Today: #_____

Week 2

> Thank God for the most precious of all gifts—the grace that enables you to say from the bottom of your heart, and with the most intense conviction: "I believe in God, the Father Almighty, Creator of heaven and earth." Pray that you may always persevere in this **FAITH**, our beacon-light in the storms of life and the best assurance of a happy death and a blissful eternity. Pray: "My God, I believe in You."

I Pray Today: #____

Day 8

My Battles Today:

_____
_____
_____
_____
_____
_____

My Sacrifices Today: #_____

_____
_____
_____
_____
_____
_____
_____

Week 2

> The virtue of **HOPE** must accompany you on your way through life. Like a **HELMET** of steel, this virtue must guard your head against the blows of fate, which are often so hard. Hope must be your protection.

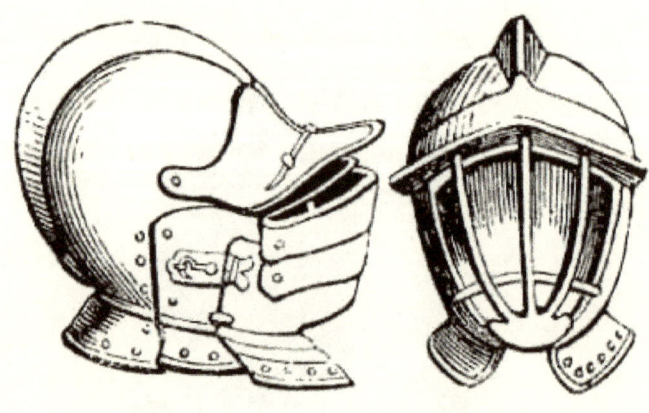

I Pray Today: #_____

_____
_____
_____
_____
_____

Day 9

My Battles Today:

My Sacrifices Today: #_____

Week 2

> ". . .let us be sober, putting on the breastplate of faith and love and the helmet that is hope for salvation." (1 Thessalonians 5:8) You must keep a firm hold on Christian HOPE; you must cling to it, and never let it go, for such is the will of God. Pray: "My God, I hope in You."

I Pray Today: # _____

Day 10

My Battles Today:
_____
_____
_____
_____
_____
_____
_____

My Sacrifices Today: #_____
_____
_____
_____
_____
_____
_____
_____

Week 2

> *"Trust in the Lord with all your heart,*
> *on your own intelligence rely not.*
> *In all your ways be mindful of him,*
> *and he will make straight your paths."*
> (Proverbs 3:5-6)

I Pray Today: # _____

_____

_____

_____

_____

_____

_____

Day 11

My Battles Today:

My Sacrifices Today: #_____

Week 2

> "... *As I live, says the Lord* GOD, *I swear I take no pleasure in the death of the wicked man, but rather in the wicked man's conversion, that he may live.*" (Ezekiel 33:11a) It is probable that though many can and will fight God to the end and be lost, they will be far fewer than those whom He will tenderly, and in His own way, bring home to Himself.

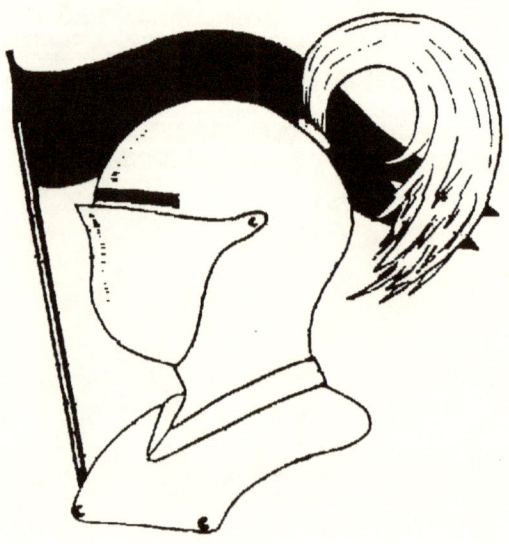

I Pray Today: #_____

Day 12

My Battles Today:

My Sacrifices Today: #_____

Week 2

> *"For the Son of Man has come to seek and to save what was lost."* (Luke 19:10) Know that your confidence in God cannot exceed His generosity that you shall never receive less than you have hoped for from Him. *"Take courage and be stouthearted, all you who hope in the LORD."* (Psalm 31:25) Pray often: "Jesus, I trust in You."

I Pray Today: # _____

Day 13

My Battles Today:

My Sacrifices Today: #_____

Week 2

> It is of the highest importance that an active, practical, abiding, unswerving **LOVE OF GOD** should dwell within your heart. If you fail in your youth to gain a mastery over the devil, the world, and the flesh, the victory will, at a later period, become very difficult —perhaps even impossible—and you will never win the heavenly crown that is the reward of him who conquers. Pray the prayer of St. Michael the archangel often.

I Pray Today:　　　　　　　　　　　　#_____

Day 14

My Battles Today:

_____
_____
_____
_____
_____
_____

My Sacrifices Today: #_____

_____
_____
_____
_____
_____
_____

Week 3

> It was LOVE that impelled God to an action neither heaven nor earth could possibly have foreseen, an action that would of itself have sufficed to justify the words of the apostle of love, *"God is love . . ."* (1 John 4:16b). Therefore, strive to free your heart from all earthly or sinful affection. Like an ARROW headed for its target, focus on loving God above all things. Ask Jesus to help you love Him above all others. Pray: "My God, I love you."

I Pray Today: #_____

_____

_____

_____

_____

_____

Day 15

My Battles Today:

My Sacrifices Today: #_____

Week 3

> What a happiness—what a joy—to be able to say to God, when this mortal life is ended, the words of the young man in the Gospel, "... *all of these* [commandments] *I have observed from my youth.*" Mark 10:20b) Therefore, make good resolutions to **LOVE GOD** in all things.

I Pray Today: #_____

Day 16

My Battles Today:

My Sacrifices Today: #_____

Week 3

> St. Paul tells us we must *"... pray at every opportunity in the Spirit."* (Ephesians 6:18) So unite yourself under the banner of LOVE, fight against the evil in this world, and earn that eternal reward that belongs to those who battle successfully in this earthly life. Tell (and show) Jesus today how much you love Him. Focus on Him alone.

I Pray Today: #_____

Day 17

My Battles Today:

My Sacrifices Today: #_____

Week 3

> "Do not grow tired . . . The days pass quickly and Jesus is drawing near."
> Sr. Agnes in a letter to Therese

I Pray Today: #_____

Day 18

My Battles Today:

My Sacrifices Today: #_____

Week 3

> An important weapon for any Christian soldier is the CROSS, for it reminds us of the love Christ has for each of us and how we must imitate that love by our **LOVE OF NEIGHBOR**. Pray: "Jesus, teach me to love as You love."

I Pray Today: #____

Day 19

My Battles Today:

My Sacrifices Today: #_____

Week 3

> Let the CROSS OF CHRIST be your banner of LOVE—the standard by which all your actions are measured. Christ commands you to *". . . 'love your neighbor as yourself.'"* (Mark 12:31) for as St. Paul says, *"If I give away everything I own . . . but do not have love, I gain nothing."* (1 Corinthians 13:3) Pray: "Jesus, help me to put others before myself."

I Pray Today: #_____

Day 20

My Battles Today:

My Sacrifices Today: #_____

Week 3

> Meditate often on the sacrifice Jesus made for you. *"'This is my commandment: love one another as I love you. No one has greater love than this, to lay down one's life for one's friends. You are my friends if you do what I command you.'"* (John 15:12-14) Pray: "Jesus, help me to love You and my neighbor by obeying your commandments."

I Pray Today: # _____

Day 21

My Battles Today:

My Sacrifices Today: #_____

Week 4

> "We must practice the little virtues. This is difficult sometimes, but the good God never refuses the first grace, which gives courage to conquer self; if the soul corresponds to it [he] will find that [he] immediately receives light. . . . We must first act with courage, then the heart is strengthened and we go from victory to victory."
> St. Therese in *Counsels and Reminiscences*

I Pray Today: #_____

Day 22

My Battles Today:

My Sacrifices Today: #_____

Week 4

> Obedience means that we subject our will to the will of another. Just as the SWORD was often the key weapon among all weapons, St. Augustine calls **OBEDIENCE** "the mother and root of all virtues." You will see that if you learn how to obey early, you will have done a great deal to promote the happiness of your future life.

I Pray Today: #_____

Day 23

My Battles Today:

_____
_____
_____
_____
_____
_____
_____

My Sacrifices Today: #_____

_____
_____
_____
_____
_____
_____
_____

Week 4

> *"He went down with them and came to Nazareth, and was obedient to them. . ."* (Luke 2:51a). Thus did Jesus Himself set the example for the virtue of **OBEDIENCE.** Consider several ways you can demonstrate the virtue of obedience. Pray: "Jesus, help me to be obedient even when it is hard."

I Pray Today: #_____

Day 24

My Battles Today:

_____
_____
_____
_____
_____
_____

My Sacrifices Today: #_____

_____
_____
_____
_____
_____
_____

Week 4

> *"If they obey and serve him [God], they spend their days in prosperity, their years in happiness. But if they obey not, they perish; they die for lack of knowledge."* (Job 36:11-12)

I Pray Today: #_____

Day 25

My Battles Today:

My Sacrifices Today: #_____

Week 4

> "See that you are preparing yourself well for the great day. You must persevere and not stop for an instant..."
>
> Sr. Agnes in a letter to Therese

I Pray Today: #_____

Day 26

My Battles Today:

My Sacrifices Today: #_____

Week 4

> The BREASTPLATE of **JUSTICE** invokes us to render to God the things that rightly belong to Him—to perform our religious duties faithfully. Among the first and foremost of these duties is the attendance at Mass on Sundays and holydays, and the suitable observance of these days in a religious spirit. But there is something more you owe Him, *"Whoever belongs to God hears the words of God. . ."* (John 8:47). Pray: "Jesus, help me to love Your words in Holy Scripture."

I Pray Today: #____

Day 27

My Battles Today:

My Sacrifices Today: #_____

Week 4

> The virtue of **JUSTICE** disposes us to give everyone what belongs to him or her. We are called to treat everyone equally. In your work and play, you must be fair to everyone and help others to act justly as well.

I Pray Today: # _____

Day 28

My Battles Today:

My Sacrifices Today: #_____

Week 5

> *"Do to others what you would have them do to you."*
> (Matthew 7:12)

I Pray Today: #_____

Day 29

My Battles Today:

My Sacrifices Today: #_____

Week 5

> Receive often the Sacraments of Reconciliation and Holy Eucharist, be truthful in word and deed, and faithful to your friends. Then this powerful BREAST-PLATE of **JUSTICE** will help gain victory for you.

I Pray Today: #_____

Day 30

My Battles Today:

My Sacrifices Today: #_____

Week 5

> Without the GIRDLE of SELF-CONTROL and self-denial, it is not possible to follow Christ for as He tell us, *"No one can serve two masters. He will either hate one and love the other, or be devoted to one and despise the other..."* (Matthew 6:24).

I Pray Today: #_____

_____

_____

_____

_____

_____

_____

Day 31

My Battles Today:

My Sacrifices Today: #_____

Week 5

> Learn how to practice self-denial and mortification. Renounce whatever is forbidden including the excessive love of pleasure (eating, entertainment, television), the lust of the flesh (impure thoughts, dread of work, idleness), and the greed of money and goods. *"Bear your share of hardship along with me like a good soldier of Christ Jesus."* (2 Timothy 2:3) What can you give up for Jesus today?

I Pray Today: # _____

_____

_____

_____

_____

_____

Day 32

My Battles Today:

My Sacrifices Today: #_____

Week 5

> Renounce first in little things, for you know that he who desires to fit himself for military service must first participate in many minor maneuvers. The same principle applies to the spiritual warfare. Without continual conquest of self, without the GIRDLE of SELF-CONTROL, no other virtue, no true happiness, can be attained. With each sacrifice, pray: "Jesus, I offer this for love of You."

I Pray Today: # _____

Day 33

My Battles Today:

My Sacrifices Today: #_____

Week 5

> Lay to heart the words of the Redeemer, *"If anyone wishes to come after me, he must deny himself and take up his cross daily and follow me."* (Luke 9:23b)

I Pray Today: #_____

Day 34

My Battles Today:

My Sacrifices Today: #_____

Week 5

> You must take upon yourself day by day the cross of **SELF-DENIAL**, of renunciation, not only in order to live an upright life, but also in order to be happy. Today, how can you follow the example of Jesus in denying yourself?

I Pray Today: #____

Day 35

My Battles Today:

My Sacrifices Today: #_____

Week 6

> "Far from being like those great souls who from their childhood practice all sorts of penances, I made my mortification consist solely in the breaking of my will, restraining a hasty word, rendering little services to those around me without making anything of it, and a thousand other things of this kind."
>
> St. Therese in *Story of a Soul*

I Pray Today:　　　　　　　　　　#_____

_____
_____
_____
_____
_____

Day 36

My Battles Today:

My Sacrifices Today: #_____

Week 6

> Among the spiritual weapons, we must include the BOW of **WORK**, which you must not connect with the idea of weariness, misery, toil, and humiliation. For work, in the proper sense of the term, includes everything that—unlike the fruit on the tree—does not come to maturity of itself. Therefore, arm yourself with this bow.

I Pray Today: #_____

Day 37

My Battles Today:

My Sacrifices Today: #_____

Week 6

> *"Go to the ant, O sluggard, study her ways and learn wisdom; For though she has no chief, no commander or ruler, she procures her food in the summer, stores up her provisions in the harvest."*
> (Proverbs 6:6-8)

I Pray Today: #_____

Day 38

My Battles Today:

My Sacrifices Today: #_____

Week 6

> Learn the right view of labor that stems from the creation of man in God's image, and work as a means in which we share in His creative activity. *"By the sweat of your face shall you get bread to eat. . ."* (Genesis 3:19). *"Six days you may labor and do all your work"* (Deuteronomy 5:13). Both of these passages indicate that work is a law of existence. Pray: "Jesus help me to work cheerfully."

I Pray Today: #_____

Day 39

My Battles Today:

_____
_____
_____
_____
_____
_____
_____

My Sacrifices Today: #_____

_____
_____
_____
_____
_____
_____
_____

Week 6

> If you remain idle and lazy, and refuse to work, you rebel against the infinitely wise law of God. Hence, it is easy to understand why the saints in all ages have been so very industrious. Never allow a single day to pass without sowing, by means of some useful work, a grain of seed in the furrows of time that may spring up and bear fruit in eternity. Learn to be faithful to your work and to regard it as honorable.

I Pray Today: # _____

Day 40

My Battles Today:

My Sacrifices Today: #_____

Week 6

> *"He put on justice as his breastplate, salvation, as the helmet on his head; He clothed himself with garments of vengeance, wrapped himself in a mantle of zeal."* (Isaiah 59: 17) It is just this MANTLE of ZEAL that dwelled in the heart of St. Paul, causing him to cooperate with the gifts of the Holy Spirit and to build up the foundations of the Catholic Church.

I Pray Today: #_____

Day 41

My Battles Today:

_____

_____

_____

_____

_____

_____

My Sacrifices Today: #_____

_____

_____

_____

_____

_____

_____

Week 6

> It is this ZEAL, as opposed to the lukewarmness of the ordinary Christian, which causes us to live lives of self-sacrifice, perform heroic works of charity, and banish all that is injurious or hostile to God and His love. *"Do not grow slack in zeal, be fervent in spirit, serve the Lord."* (Romans 12:11)

I Pray Today: #_____

Day 42

My Battles Today:

My Sacrifices Today: #_____

Week 7

> Feed your **ZEAL FOR SOULS** by receiving the sacraments frequently and living wholeheartedly the two great commandments as emphasized by Christ: *"'You shall love the Lord, your God, with all your heart, with all your soul, and with all your mind.'"* (Matthew 22:37) And *"'. . . You shall love your neighbor as yourself.'"* (Matthew 22:39) Always persevere in doing good works for the greater glory of God.

I Pray Today: #_____

Day 43

My Battles Today:

My Sacrifices Today: #_____

Week 7

> *"He shall take his zeal for armor . . ."* (Wisdom 5:17). Cloth yourself with this **ZEAL FOR SOULS** and for God's glory. Enkindle the flame of this zeal by mediating upon the Passion and Death of our beloved Savior as the intensity of zeal is proportional to that of the love felt. Pray: "Jesus, help me to love You more each day."

I Pray Today: #_____

Day 44

My Battles Today:

My Sacrifices Today: #_____

Week 7

> "You must leave nothing undone to make your heart into a heaven where Jesus will want to stay forever! Even now let this beautiful Child be the King, the love of your heart. What is there on this earth lovelier than Jesus? Jesus in His cradle, Jesus sleeping in your heart!"
>
> Sr. Agnes in a letter to Therese

I Pray Today: # _____

Day 45

My Battles Today:

My Sacrifices Today: #_____

Week 7

> *"So stand fast with your loins girded in truth . . ."* (Ephesians 6:14). Wear **TRUTH** as a BELT surrounding and securing everything you do. Hold fast to the Truth that is Jesus Christ and the Catholic Church.

I Pray Today: #_____

Day 46

My Battles Today:

My Sacrifices Today: #_____

Week 7

> *"Jesus said to him, 'I am the way and the truth and the life. No one comes to the Father except through me.'"* (John 14:6) How can you stay close to Jesus?

I Pray Today: #_____

Day 47

My Battles Today:

_____
_____
_____
_____
_____
_____

My Sacrifices Today: #_____

_____
_____
_____
_____
_____
_____

Week 7

> *"Jesus then said to those Jews who believed in him, 'If you remain in my word, you will truly be my disciples, and you will know the truth, and the truth will set you free.'"* (John 8:31-32) Love Jesus with all your heart and do all you do for His Kingdom. Let the BELT of **TRUTH** bring you salvation!

I Pray Today: _____   #_____

_____
_____
_____
_____
_____

Day 48

My Battles Today:

My Sacrifices Today: #_____

Week 7

> Another article of armor for the Catholic Christian is the ROSARY of the Blessed Virgin Mary. Arm yourself with this mighty weapon. Consecrate yourself and all your thoughts and actions to the Holy Mother of God. This virtue of **DEVOTION TO MARY** is fitting as she is the most pure Mother of our Lord and Savior. "Pray for us, O Holy Mother of God, that we may be made worthy of the promises of Christ."

I Pray Today: # _____

Day 49

My Battles Today:

My Sacrifices Today: #_____

Week 8

> "... 'Hail, favored one! The Lord is with you.'" (Luke 1:28) "... 'Most blessed are you among women, and blessed is the fruit of your womb.'" (Luke 1:42) Despite all obstacles, pray the rosary every day!

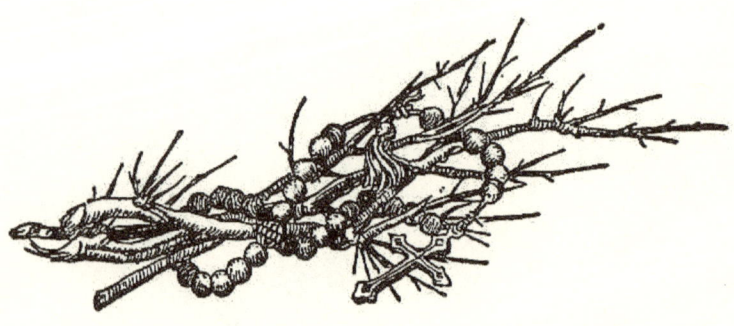

I Pray Today: #_____

_____
_____
_____
_____
_____

Day 50

My Battles Today:

My Sacrifices Today: #_____

Week 8

> The rosary is a powerful weapon against the devil. By praying the prayers of the rosary and the other prayers given to us by our Mother Mary, you are driving away the devil, releasing his hold on you. At the same time, you are honoring Jesus by honoring His Holy Mother—and our mother as well: *"Then he said to the disciple [John], 'Behold, your mother.' And from that hour the disciple took her into his home."* (John 19:27)

I Pray Today: #_____

_____

_____

_____

_____

_____

Day 51

My Battles Today:

_____
_____
_____
_____
_____
_____
_____

My Sacrifices Today: #_____

_____
_____
_____
_____
_____
_____
_____

Week 8

> *"and your feet shod in readiness for the gospel of peace."* (Ephesians 6:15) The SHOES of your armor symbolize your willingness to fight for the **PEACE OF CHRIST**.

I Pray Today: # _____

_____
_____
_____
_____
_____
_____

Day 52

My Battles Today:

My Sacrifices Today: #_____

Week 8

> Let us walk in the **PEACE OF CHRIST** confident and unafraid of anything the world can do to us for Christ tells us, *"Peace I leave with you; my peace I give to you. Not as the world gives do I give it to you. Do not let your hearts be troubled or afraid."* (John 14:27) Pray: "Jesus, help me to fight for You."

I Pray Today: #_____

Day 53

My Battles Today:
_____
_____
_____
_____
_____
_____

My Sacrifices Today: #_____
_____
_____
_____
_____
_____
_____

Week 8

Not only must the SHOES of your armor walk in the **PEACE OF CHRIST**, you must also share the gospel of Christ's peace with others. "... *'How beautiful are the feet of those who bring [the] good news!'*" (Romans 10:15). Today tell someone about Jesus.

I Pray Today: #_____

Day 54

My Battles Today:

My Sacrifices Today: #_____

Week 8

> The soldier's CHAIN MAIL reminds us that, like St. Paul, we must display **COURAGE** as disciples of Jesus and be willing to suffer ridicule, imprisonment, and even death for our Lord and King. Be inspired by St. Paul as he writes from prison, *". . . make known with boldness the mystery of the gospel for which I am an ambassador in chains, so that I may have the courage to speak as I must."* (Ephesians 6:19-20)

I Pray Today: #_____

Day 55

My Battles Today:

My Sacrifices Today: #_____

Week 8

> *"Be on your guard, stand firm in the faith, be courageous, be strong. Your every act should be done with love."* (1 Corinthians 16:13-14)

I Pray Today: #_____

_____

_____

_____

_____

_____

Day 56

My Battles Today:

My Sacrifices Today: #_____

Week 9

> "Time is passing; be courageous! Oh! If you could see the beautiful reward awaiting you! If you only knew what joy it is to have Jesus in one's heart for the first time!"
> Sr. Agnes in a letter to Therese

I Pray Today: #_____

Day 57

My Battles Today:

My Sacrifices Today: #_____

Week 9

> Just as a LANCE pierces its target, so must the **FEAR OF THE LORD** infuse your heart. Ponder deeply the words of Holy Scripture, *"The fear of the LORD is the beginning of wisdom; prudent are all who live by it . . ."* (Psalm 111:10). And *". . . to those who fear you, you are very merciful."* (Judith 16:15)

I Pray Today: #_____

Day 58

My Battles Today:

My Sacrifices Today: # _____

Week 9

> But how will you be confirmed in this **HOLY FEAR OF GOD**? By thinking upon your last end, according to the exhortation of the Holy Spirit, *"In whatever you do, remember your last days, and you will never sin."* (Sirach 7:36)

I Pray Today: #_____

Day 59

My Battles Today:

My Sacrifices Today: #_____

Week 9

> The more deeply your heart is filled with a true **FEAR OF GOD**, so much more will this fear rule and guide you in every circumstance of life, and so much less will you know any other fear, and so much more courageously will you at all times and in all places put yourself on the side of God before the eyes of the world. *"Therefore, since we know the fear of the Lord, we try to persuade others ..."* (2 Corinthians 5:11).

I Pray Today: #_____

Day 60

My Battles Today:

My Sacrifices Today: #_____

Week 9

> Keep in mind the maxim that has caused the conversion of so many sinners, and made so many saints—the memorable maxim that was spoken by Jesus Christ Himself, *"What profit is there for one to gain the whole world and forfeit his life?"* (Mark 8:36). Ask Jesus to help you fear sin and put the things of heaven before the things of this world.

I Pray Today: #_____

Day 61

My Battles Today:

My Sacrifices Today: #_____

Week 9

> The BATTLE-AX reminds us that we must separate ourselves from the things of this world, set ourselves apart from the world. To increase your **DESIRE FOR HEAVEN**, constantly turn your thoughts and attention to God and to prayer, focusing on your end goal—heaven. *"Rejoice and be glad, for your reward will be great in heaven."* (Matthew 5:12)

I Pray Today: #_____

Day 62

My Battles Today:

My Sacrifices Today: #_____

Week 9

> "'Do not let you hearts be troubled. You have faith in God; have faith also in me. In my Father's house there are many dwelling places. If there were not, would I have told you that I am going to prepare a place for you? And if I go and prepare a place for you, I will come back again and take you to myself, so that where I am you also may be.'" (John 14:1-3)
> Pray: "Jesus, help me to fix my eyes on heaven."

I Pray Today: #_____

_____

_____

_____

_____

_____

Day 63

My Battles Today:

My Sacrifices Today: #_____

Week 10

> Just as GLOVES protect the hands of the soldier, so does God's MERCY protect and provide salvation to those who love Him. As we are all sinners, without God's mercy, none would be saved. *"For the Son of Man has come to seek and to save what was lost."* (Luck 19:10) Pray: *"O God, be merciful to me a sinner."* (Luke 18:13b)

I Pray Today: #_____

_____
_____
_____
_____
_____

Day 64

My Battles Today:

My Sacrifices Today: #_____

Week 10

> But the protection of God's **MERCY** will only be given to us, if we—in turn—are merciful to others. Jesus tells us, *"Blessed are the merciful, for they will be shown mercy."* (Matthew 5:7) Pray: "Forgive us our trespasses, as we forgive those who trespass against us." (See Matthew 6:12.)

I Pray Today: #_____

Day 65

My Battles Today:

_____
_____
_____
_____
_____
_____

My Sacrifices Today: #_____

_____
_____
_____
_____
_____
_____

Week 10

A HORSE allows a soldier to persevere in battle longer than if on foot. **PRAYER** acts as our horse, propelling us toward our goal, giving us strength to persevere to the end. *"Persevere in prayer, being watchful in it with thanksgiving. . ."* (Colossians 4:2). Pray: "Jesus, You are my strength!"

I Pray Today: #____

Day 66

My Battles Today:

_____
_____
_____
_____
_____
_____
_____

My Sacrifices Today: #_____

_____
_____
_____
_____
_____
_____
_____

Week 10

HORSE and rider often become one, working closely together. So too must we become one with Christ, working with Him to accomplish His Kingdom on earth. Speak to Jesus often in **PRAYER**; study His words in Holy Scripture. *"If you remain in me and my words remain in you, ask for whatever you want and it will be done for you."* (John 15:7) Pray: "Jesus, make me one in You!"

I Pray Today: #_____

_____
_____
_____
_____
_____
_____

Day 67

My Battles Today:

My Sacrifices Today: #_____

Week 10

> Like a soldier's HORSE, our **PRAYER** to Jesus steadies us and assures us of victory. *"To the one who is able to keep you from stumbling and to present you unblemished and exultant, in the presence of his glory, to the only God, our savior, through Jesus Christ our Lord be glory, majesty, power, and authority from ages past, now, and for ages to come. Amen."* (Jude 24-25) Pray: "Glory be to the Father, and to the Son and to the Holy Spirit!"

I Pray Today: #_____

Day 68

My Battles Today:

_____
_____
_____
_____
_____
_____
_____

My Sacrifices Today: #_____

_____
_____
_____
_____
_____
_____
_____

Week 10

> "If everything is ready for the great day, you may be sure that Jesus will not come empty handed ... If you only knew what treasures are hidden in the tiny Host for a well-prepared First Communion!"
> Sr. Agnes in a letter to Therese

I Pray Today: #_____

Day 69

My Battles Today:

My Sacrifices Today: #_____

My First Communion Journal

How to Make Sacrifice Beads

Materials:
- 10 pony beads
- 1 cross, approximately 1¼"
- 1 religious medal, approximately 1"
- 22" piece of waxed string

1. You will need to attach your medal to the center of the string. Fold the string in half and pass the fold through the ring on the medal; then pass the two loose ends of the string through the loop. Now your medal is secured to the center of the string.
2. Take your first pony bead and thread it onto the string by passing one end of the string through the hole in the pony bead and the other end of the string through the hole from the opposite side of the bead.
3. The string that came out the left side of bead #1 should pass back through the hole in bead #2 from left to right and the string that exited bead #1 on the right should be passed through bead #2 from right to left.
4. Repeat step #3 for the eight remaining beads.
5. Once all ten beads are on the string, knot the two loose ends of the string together.
6. Finally, attach the cross in the same way the medal was attached to the other end. To do this, pass the knot-ted end through the loop ring (hole) in the cross then pass the opposite end of the string (the end with the medal and beads on it) through this loop and pull taut.

To use: Start with all the beads at one end. Each time you make any sacrifice, slide one bead down to the opposite end. By keeping the beads with you all the time, it will serve as a reminder to make sacrifices as St. Therese did to honor Jesus' great sacrifice for us.

(Used with permission from http://www.craftelf.com)

WHAT I WANT TO REMEMBER ABOUT MY FIRST HOLY COMMUNION

"In Commemoration of This Most Holy Sacrament"

Bibliography

Clarke, John, OCD., Translator. *St. Thérese of Lisieux General Correspondence, Volume 1, 1877-1890.* Washington, D.C.: Washington Province of Discalced Carmelites, Inc., 1982.

Descouvemont, Pierre and Halmuth Nils Loose. *Therese and Lisieux.* Grand Rapids, Michigan: Wm. B. Eerdmans Publishing Company, 1996.

Lasance, Reverend. Francis X. *The Young Man's Guide, Counsels, Reflections, and Prayers for Catholic Young Men.* New York, NY : Benziger Brothers, 1910.

Loyola, Mother Mary and Janet P. McKenzie. *The King of the Golden City Study Edition.* Bessemer, Michigan: Biblio Resource Publications, 2007.

Mother Agnes of Jesus, OCD. *Little Counsels of Mother Agnes of Jesus, OCD.* Parnell, Michigan: Ideal Publishing Company, 1982.

St. Thérese of Lisieux. *Story of a Soul, The Autobiography of St. Thérese of Lisieux.* Washington, D.C.: Institute of Carmelite Studies, 1976.

Other RACE for Heaven Sacramental Prep Resources

Communion with the Saints: A Family Preparation Program for First Communion and Beyond in the Spirit of St. Therese imitates St. Therese of the Child Jesus and her family who studied and prayed for sixty-nine days in anticipation of Therese's First Holy Communion. Modeling this preparation, the *Communion with the Saints* program will help any family find renewed fervor in the reception of the Eucharist. This resource includes a chapter-by-chapter study of the following four books:

- *The Little Flower, The Story of Saint Therese of the Child Jesus*—to provide the foundation of God's love for us and to encourage a desire for holiness

- *The Children of Fatima and Our Lady's Message to the World*—to show the sinfulness of our world and the need to avoid sin

- *The Patron Saint of First Communicants, The Story of Blessed Imelda Lambertini*—to inspire devotion to the Sacrament of Holy Communion

- *The King of the Golden City* by Mother Mary Loyola — to illustrate Jesus' Presence as a source of grace necessary to live a holy life

Each of the sixty-nine days of preparation includes read-aloud selections with enrichment activities, meditational readings, catechism lessons, and plenty of practical application to promote a growth in holiness and sanctity. Week-end suggestions include a list of over thirty-five family projects. The use of *My First Communion Journal* is encouraged with this program.

The King of the Golden City Study Edition is a new edition of a book that was originally published in 1921. This treasure of a book was written in response to a student's appeal for instructions along with "little stories" to help her prepare for Holy Communion. To fulfill this request, Mother Loyola of the Bar Convent in York, England, wrote a simple story that illustrates Jesus' desire to share an intimate relationship with each one of His children. This new edition contains some updated language but, quite deliberately, does not contain any pictures. Readers, as they progress through this story, will form a mental image of their King, one as unique and personal as their own relationship with Him. The study sections assist with the allegory, connect to the Bible as well as to the catechism, and explore the art of prayer in the spirit of the three Carmelite Doctors of the Church. Although written over ninety years ago for a young child, this book remains a timeless masterpiece of Catholic literature suitable for all ages. (Also available as a study guide only)

The Good Shepherd and His Little Lambs Study Edition is a simply told Catholic tale of four children who meet with their beloved aunt for "First Communion talks." More than a story, it is a First Communion primer that takes the tenets of the catechism and, through naturally-flowing conversations, relates them in the language of little ones to authentic Christian living. As Mrs. Bosch explains, "We might learn the catechism all the way through beautifully, and at the end find ourselves still very stiff and clumsy about loving our Lord. When He comes to us, we don't want to welcome Him into our souls only with answers out of the catechism, do we?" Enriched by appropriate Biblical passages, points of doctrine, and prayers, this story-primer is an enjoyable and effective read-aloud that will prepare the Good Shepherd's little lambs to worthily receive Him in the Holy Eucharist.

A Reconciliation Reader-Retreat: Read-Aloud Lessons, Stories, and Poems for Young Catholics Preparing for Confession provides a basic doctrinal explanation and review of the Sacrament of Reconciliation as well as

Other RACE for Heaven Resources

a Gospel examination of conscience—a seven-day read-aloud formation retreat. To help the lessons come alive and to enable young Catholics to more readily apply these doctrines to their own daily lives, the lessons have been supplemented with pertinent short stories and poems. Each lesson contains reflection questions, a family prayer, and a "Gospel Examination of Conscience" that is formulated according to the dictates of the *Catechism of the Catholic Church*. This reader-retreat will not only enrich and deepen the sacramental experience for each member of your family but it will also provide several tools to help you recommit to leading a virtuous life and to grow together in holiness.

The Outlaws of Ravenhurst Study Edition contains a classic story of the persecution of Scottish Catholics that was first written in 1923 and was revised and reprinted in 1950. This 2009 edition of Sr. M. Imelda Wallace's *Outlaws of Ravenhurst* contains the revised story of 1950 plus chapter-by-chapter aids to assist readers in assimilating the book's strong Catholic elements into their own lives. The study section focuses on critical thinking, integration of biblical teachings, and the study of the virtuous life to which Christ calls us as mature Catholics. With its emphasis on virtues (theological and moral plus the gifts and fruits of the Holy Spirit), the spiritual and corporal works of mercy, and the Beatitudes, *Outlaws of Ravenhurst Study Edition* is a fun and effective catechetical tool for Catholics preparing for the Sacrament of Confirmation. (Also available as a study guide only)

The Family that Overtook Christ Study Edition: The Story of the Family of St. Bernard of Clairvaux is an excellent read for young adults who are preparing to receive the Sacrament of Confirmation. In this exciting chronicle of the life of twelfth-century knights, we have an entire family of nine saints who lay before us their individual means of achieving intimate union with Christ. Learn with the Fontaines family how to supernaturalize the natural, develop a

My First Communion Journal

God-consciousness, and attain sanctity by being yourself. Perfect for high-school read-aloud (or adult study), this new study edition has over 250 footnotes for increased comprehension and provides discussion/meditation points to promote the art of spiritual conversation. The appendix lists formulas of Catholic doctrine that are essential for confirmands not only to know but also to incorporate into their own spiritual lives.

A Confirmation Reader-Retreat: Read-Aloud Lessons, Stories and Poems for Young Catholics utilizes chapters from two excellent out-of-print Catholic books for children (*I Belong to God, Great Truths in Simple Stories for Children and Lovers of Children* by Lillian Clark; and *Children's Retreats in Preparation for First Confession, First Holy Communion, and Confirmation* by Rev. P.A. Halpin). This book provides a basic doctrinal review of the Sacrament of Confirmation as well as prayer experiences—a nine-day read-aloud retreat/novena. The reprinted material has been supplemented with short stories and poems that provide insights in applying catechetical doctrines to the daily life of young Catholics. Each lesson concludes with "I Talk with God"—a section that encourages readers (of all ages) to deepen their relationship with each of the Three Persons of the Blessed Trinity. Reflection questions promote the habit of spiritual conversation within your family—to encourage family members to discuss holy topics—and to help you grow together in holiness. Additionally, a traditional novena to the Holy Spirit is included.

To Order: Email info@RACEforHeaven.com or place an order from RACEforHeaven.com. Discover, MasterCard, VISA, PayPal, American Express, checks, and money orders are accepted.

www.ingramcontent.com/pod-product-compliance
Lightning Source LLC
LaVergne TN
LVHW011421080426
835512LV00005B/193